Spooky Spots

SPOOKY CEMETERIES

ELSIE OLSON

Big Buddy Books

An Imprint of Abdo Publishing
abdobooks.com

abdobooks.com

Published by Abdo Publishing, a division of ABDO, PO Box 398166, Minneapolis, Minnesota 55439.

Printed in the United States of America, North Mankato, Minnesota
052020
092020

THIS BOOK CONTAINS RECYCLED MATERIALS

Design: Sarah DeYoung, Mighty Media, Inc.
Production: Mighty Media, Inc.
Editor: Liz Salzmann

Cover Photograph: Shutterstock Images
Interior Photographs: Ben Churchill/Flickr, p. 18; John W. Iwanski/Flickr, pp. 6 (Bachelor's Grove), 25; Kaspar C/Flickr, pp. 6 (Chase Vault), 23; Library of Congress, p. 20; Marcus Cyron/Wikimedia Commons, pp. 7 (Westminster Hall), 27; nikoretro/Flickr, p. 29 (backscatter); Shutterstock Images, pp. 4–5, 6, 7, 8, 9, 10–11, 13, 15, 17, 19, 21, 28 (all), 29; Wikimedia Commons, p. 12
Design Elements: Shutterstock Images

Library of Congress Control Number: 2020931821

Publisher's Cataloging-in-Publication Data
Names: Olson, Elsie, author.
Title: Spooky cemeteries / by Elsie Olson
Description: Minneapolis, Minnesota : Abdo Publishing, 2021 | Series: Spooky spots | Includes online resources and index
Identifiers: ISBN 9781532193316 (lib. bdg.) | ISBN 9781098211950 (ebook)
Subjects: LCSH: Haunted places--Juvenile literature. | Ghosts--Juvenile literature. | Cemeteries--Juvenile literature. | Spirits--Juvenile literature.
Classification: DDC 133.12--dc23

CONTENTS

HAUNTED CEMETERIES

Do you believe there are ghosts among us? Many people do. Whether you're a believer or not, cemeteries are some of the spookiest spots around!

Get ready to **explore** some of the most haunted cemeteries on Earth. Walk between the broken gravestones. Discover the secrets of hidden **tombs**. But look out! You may not be alone.

Cemeteries are even spookier at night!

World's Spookiest CEMETERIES

Are you ready for a ghostly adventure? Then pack up your wits and your **courage**. Let's take a trip to some of the world's spookiest cemeteries!

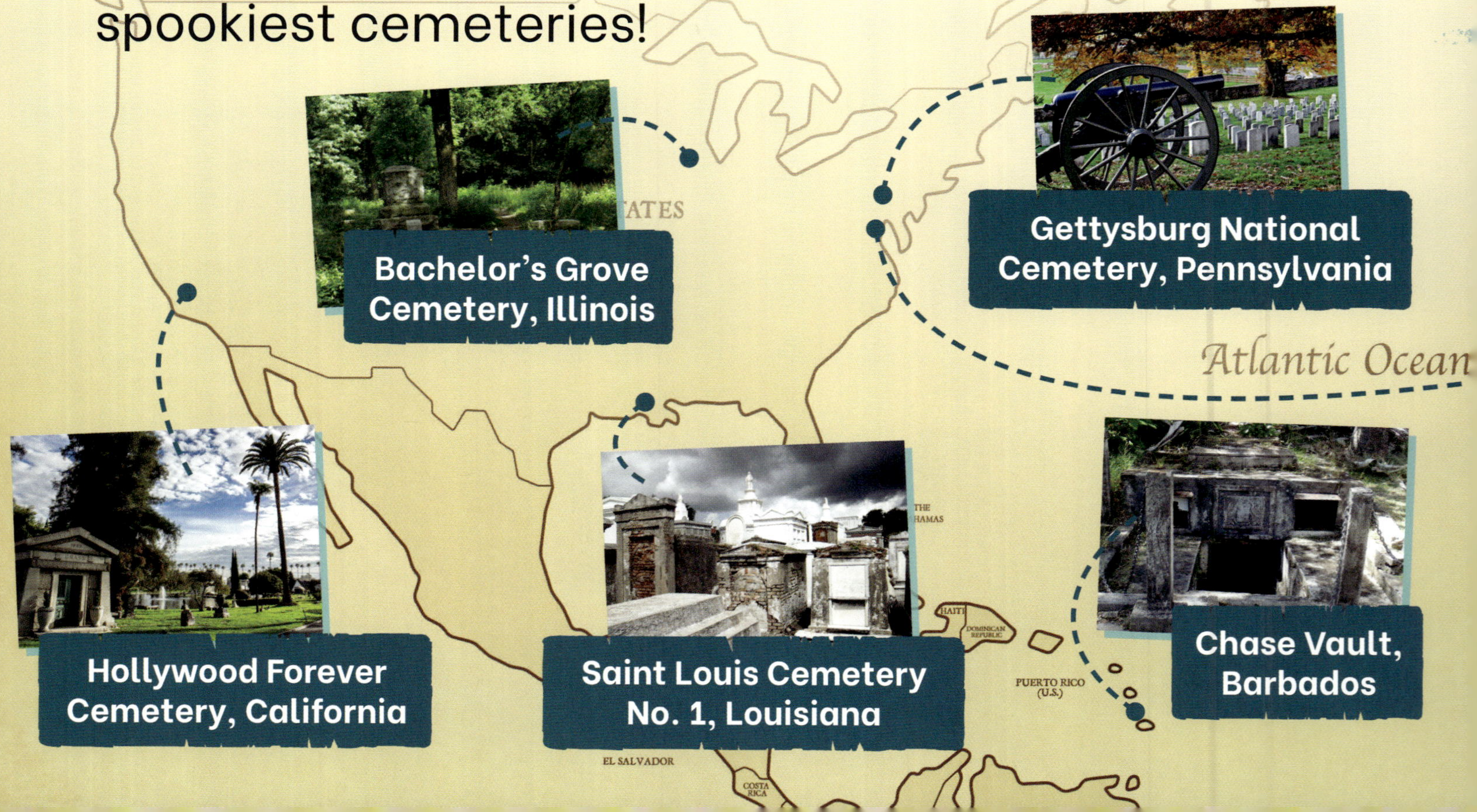

Highgate Cemetery, England
Paris Catacombs, France
Westminster Hall and Burying Ground, Maryland
N
NE
E
SE
S
SW
W
NW
MONGOLIA
CHINA
INDIA
Indian Ocean
UKRAINE
BELARUS
POLAND
GERMANY
FRANCE
SPAIN
PORTUGAL
ITALY
ROMANIA
BULGARIA
TURKEY
SYRIA
IRAQ
IRAN
AFGHANISTAN
PAKISTAN
TURKMENISTAN
UZBEKISTAN
KYRGYZSTAN
NEPAL
MYANMAR (BURMA)
LAOS
THAILAND
CAMBODIA
VIETNAM
PHILIPPINES
INDONESIA
SRI LANKA
MOROCCO
ALGERIA
LIBYA
MALI
NIGER
CHAD
MAURITANIA
WESTERN SAHARA
SENEGAL
GUINEA
BURKINA FASO
NIGERIA
GHANA
BENIN
TOGO
CAMEROON
GABON
DEMOCRATIC REPUBLIC OF THE CONGO
TANZANIA
ANGOLA
ZAMBIA
ZIMBABWE
NAMIBIA
BOTSWANA
MOZAMBIQUE
MADAGASCAR
TIMOR LESTE

HIGHGATE CEMETERY

Highgate Cemetery is in London, England. It opened in 1839. According to **legend**, the cemetery is home to the Highgate **Vampire**.

The vampire is believed to be a **nobleman** who was buried at Highgate. He is said to walk the grounds at night. Over the years, many people have tried to catch the vampire. But so far, no vampire has been caught.

More than 170,000 people are buried at Highgate.

SAINT LOUIS CEMETERY NO. 1

Many people think New Orleans, Louisiana, is one of the most haunted US cities. So, it makes sense that it has a haunted cemetery! Saint Louis Cemetery No. 1 is the city's oldest operating cemetery. It was founded in 1789.

The only way to visit the cemetery today is on a tour. And there is plenty to see there, including more than 700 **tombs**. But be aware! It seems not all of the cemetery's spirits are resting quietly.

New Orleans is below sea level. This means water is very near the land's surface. So, nearly all graves in the city are above ground.

This cemetery's most famous spirit is that of Marie Laveau. Laveau was a **voodoo** queen who lived in the 1800s. In life, she used her abilities to heal people. But some people believe her powers reach beyond the grave.

Some cemetery visitors report feelings of being touched. Others say they hear voices coming from inside Laveau's **tomb**. Some people even become ill after visiting!

FRIGHTFUL FACT

It is said that if you mark Laveau's tomb with three *X*'s, she will grant you a wish. But if the wish comes true, you must return to leave a gift at her tomb.

Laveau's tomb with gifts from grateful wishers

PARIS CATACOMBS

By the 1700s, cemeteries in Paris, France, had become too full. People complained about the smell of rotting bodies. Then in 1780, heavy rains caused the wall of a cemetery to fall. This allowed bodies to spill out of the graveyard.

So, many bodies were moved to former mining tunnels. These tunnels became the Paris **catacombs**. The catacombs run for 200 miles (322 km). In some areas, the tunnel walls are lined with human bones. Visitors have reported hearing voices. Others have seen strange shadows and floating **orbs**!

Just one mile (1.6 km) of the Paris catacombs is open to visitors.

FRIGHTFUL FACT

More than 6 million people are buried in the Paris catacombs. The oldest bodies are more than 1,200 years old!

GETTYSBURG NATIONAL CEMETERY

A famous **American Civil War** battle occurred at Gettysburg, Pennsylvania. Between 7,000 and 10,000 soldiers were killed during this battle. Afterward, 3,500 of them were buried in the battlefield. Visitors report seeing unexplained floating lights. Others report seeing strange figures in pictures taken there.

FRIGHTFUL FACT

Gettysburg National Cemetery became a national cemetery on November 19, 1863. At its opening, President Abraham Lincoln gave the Gettysburg Address. It became one of his most famous speeches.

Some visitors to Gettysburg National Cemetery have reported seeing strange figures in uniforms who disappear.

HOLLYWOOD FOREVER CEMETERY

The Hollywood Forever Cemetery is in Los Angeles, California. It was founded in 1899. The cemetery is the final home of hundreds of famous people. These include actress Judy Garland and Mel Blanc, who was the voice of cartoon character Bugs Bunny.

FRIGHTFUL FACT

The Hollywood Forever Cemetery has a monument to Terry. Terry was the dog who played Toto in *The Wizard of Oz*!

People can still purchase burial plots in the Hollywood Forever Cemetery.

The cemetery is a popular **tourist site**. It holds movie nights in the summer and daily tours. But it has spooky activities as well.

Visitors have reported seeing a woman sobbing by a lake on the cemetery grounds. Others have seen odd figures in old-fashioned clothing. People have even seen strange lights floating around the cemetery.

FRIGHTFUL FACT

Actor Clifton Webb was buried in a mausoleum at Hollywood Forever Cemetery. People have reported hearing whispers and smelling cologne in the mausoleum. Could these be from Webb's ghost?

Each year, Hollywood Forever Cemetery holds a ceremony for *Día de Los Muertos*. This is Spanish for "Day of the Dead."

CHASE VAULT

The island of Barbados is home to the Christ Church **Parish** Church Cemetery. In 1724, a **vault** was built in the cemetery. In 1808, the Chase family bought the vault and started using it.

In 1812, the vault was opened for another burial. The three **coffins** inside the vault had been tossed around!

The vault was reopened three times over the next eight years. Each time, the coffins had moved. Locals blamed an angry spirit. By then, the Chase family had had enough. They buried the coffins in another part of the cemetery.

Today Chase Vault is empty. But could a spirit remain?

BACHELOR'S GROVE CEMETERY

A graveyard near Chicago, Illinois, is believed to be one of the most haunted US cemeteries. Bachelor's Grove Cemetery is in a forest area. No one has been buried there for many years. But it is far from peaceful.

The land was set aside for burials in the 1800s. Today, visitors report seeing strange **orbs** of blue light. Others have seen a ghostly farmer and his horse. Some have even seen a farmhouse that disappears as you get close to it!

FRIGHTFUL FACT

According to **legend**, **gangsters** in the 1920s hid dead bodies and guns in Bachelor's Grove Cemetery.

Bachelor's Grove Cemetery is a popular location for local ghost hunters.

WESTMINSTER HALL AND BURYING GROUND

Westminster Hall and Burying Ground is in Baltimore, Maryland. The land has been a cemetery since 1786. In 1852, a church was built over the cemetery. It's said that people were buried alive in the cemetery and their spirits wander the grounds.

The cemetery is also home to the Cambridge **Skull**. This is the head of a murdered **minister**. **Legend** says it was covered in **cement** to stop if from screaming. But some people claim to still hear screams from the covered skull!

Visitors to Westminster Hall can tour the church and burying ground.

FRIGHTFUL FACT

Famous author Edgar Allan Poe was buried at Westminster Hall and Burying Ground in 1849. Some people say they have seen his ghost! Poe wrote many spooky stories and poems.

SPOOKY OR SCIENCE?

You've just learned about some spooky cemeteries. The creepy stories are fun! But good **explorers** look for reasons for what they see and hear. Strange happenings can often be explained by science.

Do you think the cemeteries in this book are actually haunted? You might have to visit them to find out!

IMAGINATION

Humans have excellent imaginations. Just hearing about a scary sight can trick your brain into thinking you've seen it too!

SPOOKY PICTURES

Many visitors to haunted places report balls of light in their pictures. These are likely backscatter. Backscatter is when a camera's flash lights up specks of dust or water.

NATURAL EXPLANATION

Many strange occurrences may actually have scientific explanations. For example, Barbados is in an area known for earthquakes. Could earthquakes have caused the coffins in Chase Vault to move?

EXAGGERATION

Tourist sites may exaggerate spooky stories. They hope this will make more people want to visit.

GLOSSARY

American Civil War – the war between the Northern and Southern states from 1861 to 1865.

catacomb – an underground place where people are buried.

cement – a hard, rocklike material used in buildings and roads.

coffin – a box a dead person is put in before being buried.

cologne (cuh-LONE) – a scented liquid that people put on their skin to smell good.

courage – strength or bravery.

earthquake (UHRTH-kwayk) – a shaking of a part of the earth.

exaggerate (ihg-ZA-juh-rayt) – to make something seem larger or more impressive.

explore – to go into in order to make a discovery or to have an adventure. A person who explores is an explorer.

gangster – a member of a group of criminals.

legend – an old story that many people believe but cannot be proven true.

mausoleum – a large tomb that is usually stone and above ground.

minister – a person who leads church worship.

nobleman – a member of a family that is considered important by society.

orb – something that is shaped like a ball.

parish – a small area that has its own government.

skull – the bony part of the head that protects the brain.

speck – a tiny dot or particle.

tomb (TOOM) – a special building or structure that houses the dead.

tourist site – a place people visit while on vacation.

vampire – a made-up monster that is a dead person who comes out at night to suck the blood of living people.

vault – a type of burial chamber.

voodoo – a religion that started in Haiti.

ONLINE RESOURCES

Booklinks
NONFICTION NETWORK
FREE! ONLINE NONFICTION RESOURCES

To learn more about spooky cemeteries, please visit **abdobooklinks.com** or scan this QR code. These links are routinely monitored and updated to provide the most current information available.

INDEX